LOST IDENTITY

MEMOIR OF A WORLD WAR II EVACUEE

Alice Griffin

First published 2008

ISBN 978-1-905327-15-7

For my grandchildren, Eleanor, Edward,
Georgina and Sophie. For making your parents
as proud of you as I am of them.

Contents

COVER PHOTOGRAPHS: Top: Princes Street, Deptford by kind permission of Lewisham Local History and Archives Centre. Bottom: View from Cilmanharen Farm

Acknowledgements

Andrew Tyler, writer and director of Animal Aid for his expert guidance and encouragement. For proof-reading my script and recommending it for publication. Dr Glenn Lyons for suggesting many worthwhile improvements. Precious moments spent with my granddaughter, Eleanor, whose enthusiasm propelled me to the final page. My husband Maurice for sharing in my life for 56 years. Sue Hughes and Joan Court - my soul mates, who are always there for me when dark clouds descend. All my dear friends in the animal protection movement whose compassion has never wavered.
And most of all, my two daughters, Jill and Lisa, without whom I would never have discovered my true worth.

1

WWII Evacuation

I can still recall the sound of my mother's head hitting the wall as my father vented his anger. My two sisters and I would cling to each other in the corner of the room until the shouting and violence had stopped. Doris was six, I was four and Jessie was two. We accepted this as normal family life until the outbreak of the Second World War a year later when we were to be evacuated to South Wales from Deptford in South East London. I feel compelled to write this memoir, partly as a sort of therapy, but mostly to give my grandchildren an insight into a world in which they, in their cosseted and loving family life, can only imagine or read about. It has been a journey of highs and lows and is preserved through the eyes of a small child. It is a journey I am glad to have experienced even though, like many children who have been repeatedly fostered and deprived of a loving family life, one is left with the feeling of rejection and lost identity.

For the next six years, when all three of us were evacuated at the start of the Second World War, my sisters and I were to be spared further encounters with domestic violence. No more dreading the key in the door or the footsteps on the stairs as our father staggered home from the pub. My mother would struggle to put food on the table while he willingly handed over precious house keeping money to impress his mates in the pub. He was a short stocky man for whom I had no feelings for one way or the other. Jessie and I visited him in hospital as he lay dying of a heart attack at the age of 61. I remember him saying "look after your mother". What did he know about looking after anyone? Was he asking us to make amends for all the years he neglected and abused her? Any other memories of him are best left unrecorded.

I don't know anything about my parents' history except that I was told my mother came from Ireland with her parents and a vast number of siblings of whom she was the youngest. I imagine she was at the bottom of the pecking order receiving little education or loving attention. She hardly ever talked about her family except on one occasion, many years later, when it was raised in conversation. Her face changed and took on a look of anxiety and irritation. It was obvious she did not want to talk about it. I never knew her to have friends or mix with anyone outside the home. She was pretty with long black hair and green Irish eyes but sadly, unlike the song, I never saw them smile.

Unfortunately the hostility and violence was to resurface when my sisters and I returned home from Wales after the war. But this time it was my mother delivering the blows. On our return she appeared kindly at first and I willingly handed over the £2.16.3d, that I had saved during my stay as an evacuee on an isolated farm in the Welsh hills, with the promise that she would pay me back. Being miles away from shops in Wales there was nothing to spend it on so my savings slowly grew and every now and again I would count them and imagine what I would buy when I grew up.

Some of the money was given to me by men who came to our farm to rent a day's shooting. As they stood there at the end of the shoot, their guns tucked nonchalantly under their arms, I waited patiently, anticipating a reward for them being allowed on to our land to shoot. I glanced at the dead rabbits that they had shot, dripping blood, their little furry lifeless bodies dangling like catkins from a hazel tree, their eyes open and glazed. I accepted this as quite normal on a working farm but as time went on and I was to witness appalling, habitual cruelty, that I now see as inherent in most livestock farming, I became disturbed by what I saw and I slowly developed an empathy with all the farm animals which was to stay with me all my life.

2

A long goodbye

Time came for us to be sent from the dangers of Hitler's bombs to the protection of the countryside. My two sisters and I, and later another two sisters, were some of the 1.5 million children who were evacuated, mostly unaccompanied, to live with strangers in various parts of the country considered to be safe. We arrived at school with our belongings stuffed into pillow cases. There were about a hundred children in all. Most were from poor families like us, looking slightly unkempt; coats too short or too long, socks hanging over downtrodden shoes and an ill assortment of luggage bags. In contrast, the better-off kids were smartly dressed with proper suitcases in which I imagine nice clothes were neatly packed with a view to reminding future foster parents that the children came from a respectable family and should be treated accordingly.

Amidst a lot of noise and commotion we were immediately put into a line to have identity labels pinned or tied to our coats and belongings. When everyone was ready, accompanied by some of our teachers, we clambered on to buses that took us to the railway station. Tin boxes containing gas masks were hung around our necks. We were shown how to put them on and I can remember panicking because I thought I would not be able to breathe. Jessie became hysterical with fear which started everyone else crying. Finally, as I looked through the perspex window of the gasmask at other children wearing them I thought how frightening they looked. They would surely put the fear of God into anyone who came within a hundred yards of us.

However, like most things that had suddenly intruded upon our young lives we soon got used to them.

As we scrambled off the buses at the railway station, trying desperately to hold on to our belongings, being pushed and shoved in all directions, I started to worry about what on earth was happening to us. There were children everywhere, some crying, some visibly excited about the prospect of an impending adventure, some clinging to adults, others just looking lost and bewildered. I looked at Doris for reassurance but she looked as frightened as I was.

Not many of us had ever been to a railway station or seen the gigantic machines puffing out steam like huge dragons and every now and again letting out such a terrifying hiss that we clung to each other in fear. As we were ushered once again into an orderly line stretching back as far as the eye could see, the noise seemed to get louder as one of the trains began to heave itself out of the station. Hundreds of little hands were waving from the windows as parents appeared to fall silent, maybe realising that they would not see their children again for a long time.

The remaining children moved slowly towards a long line of tables behind which stood women in green uniforms, who I later learned were from the Women's Royal Voluntary Service, the 'much admired' WRVS as they were always known. They smiled at us reassuringly and gave each one of us a big brown paper bag. I pulled myself up on tiptoe and took a bag. Doris took one for herself and one for Jessie who could hardly see over the top of the table. As we peered inside the bags we soon forgot our fears. We couldn't believe our eyes. There were biscuits, chocolate, fruit, a tin of evaporated milk and things that we had never seen before. I clutched the bag tightly and my mouth began to water. Mrs. Jennings, one of the teachers who accompanied us, was busy checking her charges and tapped each one of us on the shoulder as she counted to see if we were all present and correct. When she was satisfied she ushered us onto a platform where our train awaited. Porters were on hand to help the little ones up onto the train, with words of comfort that we are going on a nice long journey and everything was going to be all right. As Jessie was being lifted onto the train she dropped her bag of goodies and began to scream, fearing that it was lost forever, but the porter picked it up and put it into her hand, wrapping her little fingers around it as he comforted her. We found our seats and climbed up to look out of the windows. People were standing on the platform, mostly women but a few men as well. Some were waving goodbye as they fought back the tears, others were crying and sobbing openly which started me off as well although I didn't know why I was upset except maybe the fear of the unknown. There must be something wrong if all those people were crying.

As the train steamed out of London on into the open countryside we soon settled down and began to enjoy the journey. Everyone was investigating the contents of their goodie bags, making sure that no one had got more than them. Mouths were being stuffed with chocolate and biscuits. Jessie had managed to get chocolate everywhere except in her mouth and Mrs Jennings was busy trying to clean her up. The thought of having the chocolate taken away sent her into hysterics until Mrs Jennings relented and turned to supervise the next child.

Doris and Jessie and I were some of the first evacuees to leave London and our first port of call was Hastings where we were to be billeted with an elderly couple, Mr and Mrs Smith, in a little back-to-back terrace house. I don't remember much about it except that all three of us slept together in one big bed.

One day a woman came and gave each of us a toy. I had a blue teddy bear that I called Bobby. I treasured him for years. Jessie had a big Sally doll that I was very jealous of. I don't remember what Doris had. We used to go to a nearby shop and buy black liquorice bars which were called golly bars (not politically correct now) and toffee bars that cost a farthing each. Also little sweets like gobstoppers that changed colour as you sucked them and when you got to the end there was a little aniseed ball. Doris managed to push one up her nose and we couldn't get it down until Mrs Smith gave her a handkerchief and told her to blow hard. It took several attempts until it eventually popped out. Not to be wasted she popped it straight back into her mouth.

Soon Hastings became the target for German bombs and it was no longer considered safe to stay there. This meant us being moved further away to the beautiful Welsh countryside which, although initially hostile and alien to us, became our salvation.

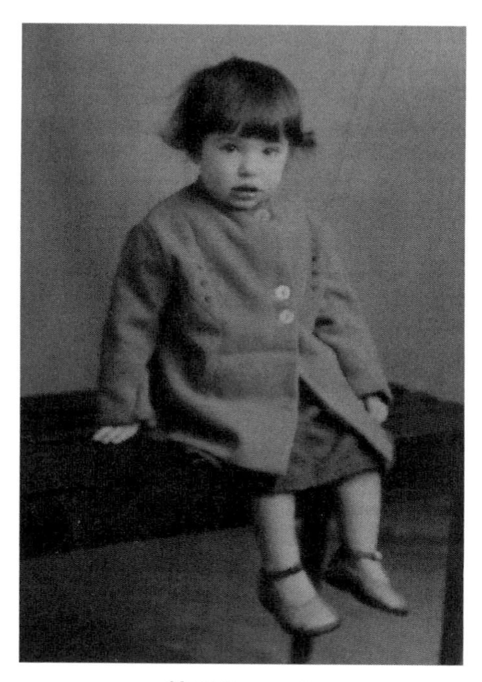

Me at 3 years old

Evacuation

3
The 'cattle market'

After another long journey the train chugged and puffed into a small railway station in a Welsh market town. As we were helped off the train, looking dazed and tired from the long journey, we were taken into a large hall. Crowds of soberly dressed women, were standing together watching as we entered the hall. A few had babies who were wrapped in large shawls that went over the mother's shoulder round her back, under her right arm, then round the baby and tucked securely underneath, leaving both hands free. Years later when I returned to Wales I saw women still carrying their babies in this way.

We were all ushered into the hall by our teachers who had accompanied us from London. 'Now, be on your best behaviour' we were told 'because you are going to be chosen by new foster parents'. As women came towards us, my two sisters and I held on to each other tightly so as not to be separated. Some of the women were talking amongst themselves in a strange tongue, others were asking questions and stating if they wanted boys or girls and how many. If they took more than one they would only take the same sex and girls were not very popular, particularly if they were around the age of puberty.

One by one, chosen children were led off with their respective foster parents until there was just a small group of children left which included my two sisters and me. Understandably, three united siblings, girls at that, were not the first choice of those with limited experience of young children aged three, five and seven who may well turn out to be quite a handful. I saw one stern looking women staring at us very intently. The tip of her nose almost reached the tip of her chin. Her hair was scraped back into a bun beneath a black woollen hat and she had a moustache which I thought was very strange. 'Please, please don't choose us' I heard myself saying. I pulled on Doris's coat and she sensed the urgency so we all held on to each other tightly and pushed our way to the back of the group of the less appealing children who were left. Jessie started crying and her nose was running profusely, mingling with her tears, which thankfully appeared to put the woman off as she turned her attention elsewhere. Eventually a kindly looking round faced woman with black rimmed glasses said she would take all three of us and as we realised that this was the best offer we were likely to get we willingly followed her to the waiting bus.

I was reminded of this episode years later as I watched animals being herded and auctioned in a livestock market in Bury St Edmunds. Little frightened creatures wondering what on earth was happening to them as they were roughly herded in all directions. I noticed one of the lorries had a South Wales name and address so these sheep had travelled hundreds of miles from the peace and tranquility of the Welsh hills and, as they clambered off the lorries into an alien, frightening world of strange noises and harsh commands my anger grew towards the callous market workers. Four men at the other end of the market were shoving and prodding a poor worn out dairy cow as they struggled to get her on to a lorry destined, I was told, for the slaughterhouse. Her udder was almost touching the ground and the back of her hind feet were split and bleeding. She had given her all, including all her babies, so she was now of no further use. As I screamed at them to stop I got the attention of people standing around, including the market inspector and the vet. At first they were more intent on trying to remove me from the market than helping the cow until other people came to my aid. I didn't save the cow but the vet told the men to leave her alone and I was ushered away by the market inspector. I noticed the words 'Spent Cattle' on one of the market sheds. That really brings home the callousness and indifference of people involved in this ruthless trade.

4
On the move again

It was a cold grey day when we arrived at Pentwyn and as we turned into the farmyard there was nothing to lift my spirits. Just a whitewashed somber-looking house surrounded by a stone wall and a muddy cobbled yard. Several skinny-looking black and white dogs came submissively towards us. Auntie Edith, as we were instructed to call her, said they would not hurt us and she introduced them to us by name, Gip, Bob and Molly. We were led into an outhouse with a stone floor and, what I was later to discover, a huge cheese press that took up one whole wall. Then on into the living room with a warm inviting fire. Old saggy armchairs and sofa had no doubt soothed the aching bones of the farm labourers after a long hard day's work in the fields. My eyes were drawn to a large table that had been previously laid for tea with a gleaming white tablecloth, silver cutlery, napkins and delicate bone china. This contrasted vividly with the drab appearance of the house exterior, as did the huge Welsh dresser that stood proud and majestic against one wall and contained lots of beautiful delicate china and other presumably valuable items.

Auntie Edith was the spinster daughter of Mr and Mrs Davies, the elderly tenants of the farm. She was quite stout and wore the regulation crossover pinafore wrapped around her that most housewives seem to wear. Strong studded lace-up boots, that echoed on the stone floors, were evidence of the harsh working conditions of farmers' wives, who often worked as hard as the men. But for all her austere appearance she was a kindly person. She had collected us from the station and had obviously been put in charge of looking after us. She took our coats and hats and proceeded to put food on the table whilst chatting away about how we must be hungry after such a long journey. There was so much food - huge lumps of cheese, delicate slices of bread and butter, cold meat, apple tart and the traditional Welsh cakes which were never absent from the table wherever one went in Wales. When we had sampled everything on the table including such unfamiliar things as faggots and brawn, we were shown how the bread, butter and cheese were made.

We were then led into another room called the pantry and to my horror we were shown where the meat came from. One whole side of a pig minus the head and feet was hanging from the ceiling. The other half was lying on a stone slab covered with salt. I felt a shudder go through my body as I noticed the pig's head lying next to it, eyes closed, pale and expressionless, and then more horror as four little feet, now pristine clean, were lying alongside, no evidence of happy days in muddy fields. I felt the urge to put all the pieces back together again. Auntie Edith must have noticed my concern and tried to reassure me that I would soon get used to it. It later became apparent that no-one, not even the smallest children, were spared the naked truth of life on a working farm. They were not intentionally cruel, but desensitisation sets in at a very early age allowing the concept to take root that farm animals have no more status than any other agricultural products.

Later, the door of the outhouse opened and an elderly man with a pronounced stoop and very bowed legs came in wiping his hands. He took off his cap and stood looking at us for some time. He smiled, displaying a few remaining discoloured teeth.

He asked each of us our names and shook our hands one

by one. His hand felt cold, rough and bony and I pulled mine away hoping he wouldn't notice my revulsion. 'My name is Jack' he said 'I am Auntie Edith's brother, I hope you are going to be happy with us.' He was a lovely kind man, never raising his voice and always ready to chat and answer our constant barrage of questions. Like many of the farmers, he chewed tobacco constantly. Now and again he would take the slimy brown ball out of his mouth and put it in his waistcoat pocket.

We had great difficulty understanding the Welsh dialect at first but before very long anyone meeting us for the first time would assume we were Welsh born and bred.

We soon settled into a well-ordered life with plenty to eat and lovely countryside in which to play and explore. We had great fun playing in a stream that ran by the side of the house and spent many hours turning over stones and watching the aquatic life swim away. Another pastime was climbing the many trees and making swings. We would walk for miles around the fields picking blackberries which Auntie Edith made into scrumptious pies or jam. We picked rosehips that we would take to school, from where they would be collected to be made into rosehip syrup for the war effort. Vast buckets of elderberries would be turned into rich ruby red wine of which Uncle Jack was very partial. Beautiful wild flowers were picked from the meadows for the living room table. Hayfields, cornfields and meadows adorned the countryside like scatter cushions and patchwork quilts. Animals grazed freely and chickens clucked and dust-bathed. Inevitably, there was cruelty but their lives were idyllic compared to today's industrialised and brutal intensive farming.

Life was sweet, but not all evacuees were so lucky. Some found being separated from their families very traumatic, especially when their foster homes were not very good, as was often the case. It came to light after the war how evacuees were often neglected and abused in some foster homes. Children were affected in different ways, but one of the results of all the upheaval was bed-wetting. I don't know if I did this prior to being evacuated but I certainly did it now.

I was routinely on the receiving end of Auntie Edith's wrath when she discovered a soggy bed and night clothes so I was made to sleep on a very uncomfortable rubber sheet. Inexperienced as she was with young children she mistakenly thought that a spell shut in the wardrobe might solve the problem. It stank of mothballs I remember. It didn't last long and she only did it once. She was not deliberately unkind and did her best to provide for us and taught us many social skills that I doubt we would have acquired at home in London. However, because of my bed wetting my stay at Pentwyn was short lived and I was packed off to a children's home in Sennybridge about twenty miles away. Doris could not settle and soon returned to London which just left Jessie at Pentwyn. I never went back there again and only saw my sister Jessie at school.

I always thought evacuees were fostered by well intentioned volunteers but I later learned that people with suitable accommodation and circumstances were encouraged to take them in and were financially rewarded.

5
Yet another move

Mary Gibbs

Still only five years old a lot has happened since boarding the train from London and I am once again on the move dragging my pillow case containing all my belongings to pastures new – a children's home in Sennybridge.

The car swung off the road through two huge stone pillars and up a wide sweeping driveway into the grounds of a very impressive looking mansion that had visibly enjoyed more affluent times. A large ornate oak door led into an inhospitable hall. My hobnailed boots reverberated on the stone floor as I was handed over to a short very rounded woman resembling a cotton reel. She appeared to roll across the floor like a wobbly ball. She led me into a large room full of boys and girls of all ages. They came running towards me intrigued to meet the newcomer. Introductions over I was given a tour of my new surroundings. Later, left to our own devices, I was to discover that one of the initiating ceremonies by the older children was to put a cushion over the newcomer's head to see how long they could hold their breath. To this day I have a fear that at some point in my life my breathing will be restricted.

When it was time for bed I was shown to a dormitory with five beds. One of the beds was on its own in an alcove which I was told was mine. There was a brass plaque on the wall with writing on it which I couldn't read but as I was climbing into bed I was informed by the other children that it said 'A famous ghost has slept in this bed and during the night rats come out and bite your neck'. When the roly poly woman came to see if we were all tucked up she found me standing outside the door sobbing. When I told her what had happened she comforted me and reassured me that they were just playing a practical joke and she took me to sleep in another room with three other girls. I later learned that the brass plaque was a memorial to a famous benefactor.

Meal times resembled a free-for-all. If it was the midday meal, plates of food were brought in and put in front of each child. The children were then left to their own devices and very often the bigger ones would help themselves to the smaller ones' food. Swede and parsnips still leave me with memories of gagging and tears rolling down my face as I was coerced into eating them. Plates of sandwiches were delivered in the same way for tea and it was a case of first come first served. Before we went to bed we had a delicious cup of Ovaltine and a biscuit.

I don't think I was in the children's home very long, just until they could find another billet for me I suppose. One day a car came to take me to another foster home several miles away from my sister at Pentwyn but at least we got to see each other at school.

6

My final move

I arrived at Cilmanharen on another wet miserable day. As the car turned off the narrow lane into the farmyard I stretched up to peer out of the window and noticed chickens, ducks and geese scurrying in all directions. I suppose it wasn't every day that their peace and tranquility were interrupted by such noisy contraptions as motor cars. Sitting in the back of the big black car I waited for Mrs Williams to open the door. My feet could barely reach the running board so she took my hand and helped me to the ground. I clutched my gasmask and Bobby, my teddy bear, and looked around at various grey stone buildings, one of which was to be my home for the next six years. Across the yard was a dirty looking pond surrounded by a few tall pine trees. It did not look a very inviting place, apart from the ducks and chickens there was no sign of life.

Mrs Williams took my hand and said 'Come on love, this is your new home now'. As this was my fourth move since leaving London such a short time ago any idea of permanency did not enter my mind.

We walked round a narrow passage that led to the back of the house and entered what was the main living room. It had a grey stone floor and a huge pine table and chairs against one wall. The only other items of furniture were two armchairs, and with just one small window, the room appeared very sparse. But there was a lovely roaring fire burning in a huge inglenook fireplace. Flames were dancing on the walls and ceiling which seemed to bring the room to life and appear warm and welcoming. Over the fire hung a big black kettle which was quietly puffing away as no doubt it did every day in preparation for an instant cup of tea. It was obvious that such necessities as hot running water had not yet arrived on these primitive hillside farms. I stood clutching Mrs Williams's hand tightly, daring her to leave me.

Looking around the room I suddenly froze. Partially hidden behind the door was a really old man sitting in an armchair. He had white hair and a long white beard. His gnarled hand was curled around an equally gnarled walking stick and he was puffing on an old clay pipe that had turned part of his white beard a dirty brown. He was wearing grey flannel trousers, a greasy looking waistcoat, a flannel shirt and big studded boots. Mrs Williams lifted me up on to an armchair opposite the old man, leaving my legs dangling like Jessie's rag doll. She said 'This is Grandad, you will be alright now love, they'll be back soon.' I didn't know who 'they' were but as she attempted to leave I tried to get down from the chair and go after her but she was gone before I could beg her not to leave me. I gave the old man a wide berth and climbed back on to the chair. I could feel my heart pounding. As I stared at him he must have sensed my fear and he took out his pipe and smiled. Unfortunately this did nothing to allay my fears. He mumbled something through his beard that I could not understand.

It seemed like an eternity before other people began to arrive, all dressed in black. The men wore black bowler hats and shiny gaiters over big black boots. They were all talking so fast I couldn't understand what they were saying until one of them said 'Oh hello, you must be Alice. You have come to live with us haven't you. Let's have a nice cup of tea and a piece of cake shall we.' She was Grandad's housekeeper and she looked after me for a while until I was sent back to the children's home in Sennybridge a second time but I can't remember why. I learned later that they had all been to a funeral. Mr Price, who I was to call Uncle Tom, was the old man's son and they were returning from his wife's funeral. It did cross my mind many years later that it was a very inopportune time to introduce a five-year old child into a new foster home.

I don't know how long I was in the children's home for the second time but when I returned to Cilmanharen Uncle Tom had married and I was introduced to Auntie Glad, his new wife. She was a lovely cultured woman. Considering she had never had children of her own she was very understanding. She never scolded me when I wet the bed or stole chocolate from the cupboard in the pantry. Instead she quietly pointed out that a piece of chocolate was meant to be a reward for doing little jobs like collecting sticks for the fire or feeding the chickens, and if I had wet the bed it would be best to let her know so she could change the sheets. I never stole anything again and I don't think it was too long before I had stopped wetting the bed. She was the nearest person I had to a mother and I kept in touch with her for a long time after returning to London. It was with great sadness that I learned of her death many years later, and whilst visiting her grave in the tiny chapel cemetery memories came flooding back of her kindness and how much I owed her for her guidance and protection. She did her best to shield me from the things she knew upset me like the cruelty to the animals because I think she secretly felt the same. There were no cuddles or kisses but then it never occurred to me to expect them so I never missed them. I was happy in my own little world of fantasy, experiencing peace of mind and the general everyday dependability of an ordered life. Children are resilient and mostly accept things as normal so I did not consciously compare the varying patterns of my life. I know I was happy most of the time.

There were no kitchens or bathrooms or inside toilets on

these isolated farms. Water was carried from an outside tap and the lavatory was in a field a short distance from the house. Chamber pots were the norm and were often very ornate. I remember there was one with a picture of a butterfly on the bottom that I refused to sit on. A wash in a tin bath was a Saturday night ritual in front of the fire and when Auntie washed my hair she would sometimes curl it with strips of rag to form ringlets. Kitchen chores were done on the big pine table including the weekly task of bread and cake making. Flour was stored in a huge bin in the pantry and I often noticed little mice droppings in it. There was a big bread oven in the wall that would be filled with wood and allowed to burn down to embers before putting the bread and cakes in to bake. The house was filled with the most delicious aroma as the weekly supply of four big loaves of bread and two large fruit cakes were taken out of the oven. Butter was made in the pantry from our own cow's milk and I often helped with pouring the milk through the separating machine to make the butter. The cream and other ingredients, that I can't remember, were then put into a big churn and sometimes I would turn the handle until it solidified. It was then weighed and formed into half pound portions. I used to love putting on the pretty patterns with special ornate spatulas before it went off to market every Friday. Uncle Tom would take a huge basket containing butter, eggs, bacon and cheese out to the main road on Chess, one of our two horses. Auntie would walk the mile or so behind and wait for the weekly bus to take her to town to sell her wares. When it was time for her to come home, the little ancient bus would stop at the school house and pick up any children, including me, who could be dropped off on his round. As Auntie and I got off the bus Uncle Tom would be waiting on Chess to help carry anything she had bought in town. There would always be a little treat for me.

On the odd occasion when we had visitors they would drool over Auntie's home made cooking. Nothing shop bought could compare with her ability to turn basic ingredients into works of art. Succulent apple pies were her specialty and would shame the most venerated chefs today. Occasional visitors would often go away with a loaf of bread, half a pound of butter and a chunk of fatty bacon. It wasn't until I returned to London that I really appreciated how lucky I had been to have had plenty of lovingly prepared food.

Cilmanharen was a working farm, mostly self sufficient, with cows, pigs, sheep, horses, chickens, ducks, geese and, of course, the faithful, highly-strung and devoted sheep dogs. At five years old and the only child living on an isolated farm high in the Welsh hills, having been previously separated from my two sisters, the animals became my main companions. I think I could tell you more about animal behaviour than all the professed experts. I knew when they were happy or sad, what they liked or disliked, and most of all when they were frightened. And when their time came they had good reason to be frightened.

One evening Uncle Tom got his gun from the cupboard in the parlour and went out of the house. Before I had time to wonder what he was going to do I heard a shot. I made for the door to go and see what had happened but Auntie gently took my hand and said, 'No bychan, come and help me make the supper.' When Uncle Tom came back I asked him what he had done. He explained that Nelly, our lovely very old sheepdog, was ill and had to be shot to save her further suffering. He left the room to put the gun back in the cupboard and it was quite some time before he came back. If animals were not 'pulling their weight' they were of no use. Pets were unheard of.

Cilmanharen was also an arable farm where fields were ploughed by our two horses and the wheat, oats and barley were cut by hand with a scythe. Harvest-time was always one of the busiest and most enjoyable times of the year when extra help was taken on, including the much admired 'land army girls'. They were very hard-working and popular with the opposite sex, particularly one big buxom blonde called Elizabeth. At lunch times it was my job to take them big chunks of bread and cheese, welsh cakes and cider, which made me feel very important. One day when the threshing was in full swing one of the hired men put his hand in the threshing machine to release some straw and the big fat needle threaded with twine used to bind the bales, went right through his hand. There was blood everywhere and he was rushed to hospital.

I would often help in the barn putting straw through the chaffing machine as Chess walked around and around in a circle outside in order to turn the wheel. When it was haymaking time I would sit on top of the horse drawn wagon and help to spread the hay evenly as it was thrown up by the farm hand. I cherished those hot sunny carefree days. What city child today could experience such delights in their materialistic concrete jungles?

I was once walking around the fields collecting blackberries when I came upon a dead rabbit in a wire snare which had embedded in her neck. I was so upset and from then on I vowed to make a point of looking for snares whenever I was out in the fields. I struggled to pull the pegs out of the ground and throw them in the hedge thus saving many defenceless creatures. I was never questioned about the possibility of being the culprit.

7
Confronting death

I was still only five years old when I arrived at Cilmanharen for the first time and was left on my own in a strange house with an old man who resembled Methuselah. I hadn't been there long before he died and I can remember going into his bedroom when no one was around to find out what a dead person looked like. I opened the door very slowly, my heart was pounding wondering what I was going to find, but I felt compelled to carry on. He was lying on the bed fully covered with a white sheet. A lone candle was burning softly, creating flashes of light and shadow, like angels floating across the room. I thought he must have gone to heaven. I held my breath, transfixed by the spooky atmosphere. I could see the outline of his nose and chin and I gave a shudder. The outline of his body looked smaller than I remember, and I recall there was a very unpleasant smell. Because I could not summon the courage to pull back the sheet I never did discover what a dead person looked like.

The old man had lived a long and fulfilled life, and had died with dignity. Everyone was grief stricken and the funeral was attended by many people, some of whom were just passing acquaintances. A feast was prepared and people gathered to reminisce about the old man's life and how he would be sadly missed.

Unfortunately non-human animals, who share many of the same characteristics as ourselves, are denied the same condolences. They are often deprived of everything that makes life worth living and are slaughtered with complete disregard for their feelings and emotions. I believe that religious teachings must accept responsibility for denying other sentient creatures the same consideration as ourselves in relation to their needs. It is all about having a soul, so they say, but what is a soul without compassion. It wasn't long before I was to realise just that.

We had one very large pig on the farm who I called Rosie. I had so much fun with her. She would squeal with joy as I chased her around the field, especially when I attempted to ride on her back briefly before she threw me off. On my return from school she would always be waiting for me the other side of the farm gate. It never ceased to surprise me how she knew the exact time I came home. As soon as she saw me she would squeal and turn round and round, her little curly tail spinning with excitement. She would love me to scratch her rough scaly back or stroke her ears. Her nose resembled a baby's bum all soft, pink and silky. I loved Rosie more than I loved any human being. She was my best friend.

One day as I sat by the fire learning to knit two men came to the house whom I recognised from a nearby farm. They were given a glass of home made cider which was always on tap in the outhouse. 'Right' said one of the men when they had finished their drink, 'Shall we get started'. I wondered what they were going to do and I followed them out into the farmyard. They made for the pigsty. I had been wondering why Rosie had been shut away instead of roaming around outside as she normally did. I was hoping they were not going to put those big metal rings in her nose again that made her squeal so much last time. Rosie came out of the sty followed by the two men. She grunted softly, her head swaying from side to side, eyes shaded by her big floppy ears. They ushered her towards the barn where I noticed Uncle Tom had gone a short time previously. I skipped along behind them asking what they were going to do but got no answer. I asked again, this time with more urgency as I tugged on one of the men's coats. "Wait, wait, what are you going to do" I begged. I don't know why I ran on into the barn and climbed up the ladder into the hay loft. I had hardly sat down on the straw, my legs dangling over the edge, when Rosie was lying on her back on a bench her squeals piercing the air. In a flash one of the men stuck a knife in her throat and her squeals turned to a gurgle as blood starting pouring out of her neck into a bucket. I can't explain how I felt. I tried to scream but no sound came. The blood seemed to drain from me just as it did from Rosie. Then I started to scream at them to stop as I stumbled back down the ladder, but of course it was too late. One of the men looked at me and smiled. 'It's all right bychan, it was all over quickly, she didn't feel a thing.' I really wanted to believe him but her screams told me otherwise. When her screams had subsided and she lay motionless they poured boiling water over her and began scraping off all her lovely bristles. In no time she was pristine clean and shiny, not at all like my lovely dirty hairy Rosie. I ran into the house to tell Auntie what they had done. I was sure she would be really angry when she knew but she quietly changed the subject and gave me a piece of chocolate from the special cupboard in the pantry.

I missed Rosie so much. My steps no longer quickened as I neared the farm gate after school and my heart sank at the sight of her empty sty. The next time I saw her she was in two halves covered in salt and lying on a cold slab in the pantry. Later, when she was sufficiently cured, half of her was hung on hooks in the living room and supplied everyone with bacon throughout the year. Anyone who happened to call at the farm to do the odd job would be given a lump of her. When I sat down to dinner one day I was given a plate of pink slimy stuff which I was told was pigs brains - Rosie's brains. All I can remember was burning my tongue so I don't think I ate it. Then there were faggots, chitlins and brawn which I ate with gusto. Someone blew up what must have been her bladder and I played football with it. How easily one forgets.

Another encounter with man's callous nature was a visit by the hunt. At the time I thought this was very special. Hunters would be given cider and Welsh cakes and they would make a great fuss of me which I revelled in. The hounds and horses would be muddy and sweating and were allowed to drink from the water trough and buckets. I was so envious of the young riders in their smart riding gear sitting proud on their coveted horses. However, one day I was to see the other side of their sordid pursuit. I heard the hunting horn some way off and ran out on to the farmyard. I was shocked to see a fox run across the yard and into the big barn followed closely by the pack of hounds. There was such a din as riders came in hot pursuit. A man sprang off his horse and ran into the barn. He came out shortly after, smiling and holding the fox by his tail. The fox was wet and muddy and frothing at the mouth. Members of the hunt were cheering and raising their glasses as he cut off his tail and threw the live fox to the hounds. I was no longer enjoying the spectacle but for fear of appearing hostile to their sport I pretended to join in their ghoulish fun. The man who had cut off the fox's tail went over to a young rider and wiped blood across both her cheeks. She looked embarrassed and, with her face dripping blood, I felt slightly sorry for her. I am now filled with revulsion whenever I see or hear about hunting, not just because of the cruelty to the fox, there is far more cruelty in meat production, but more for the way it degrades the human spirit. I will never forget the hunters visibly revelling in the brutish demise of one solitary little creature who posed no threat to them at all.

All the animals had their roles to play in the running of

the farm. Even the farm cats were assigned rat catching duties. But cat numbers were periodically controlled by drowning day old kittens in a bucket of water. I would watch the new mothers desperately searching all around the farm, calling for their young. Chickens and ducks would often appear on the table. They were killed with a knife down their throat and swung by their legs until their little bodies surrendered the last drop of blood. Young lambs were castrated without anaesthetic and their little testicles, referred to as sweetbreads, were a yearly delicacy. I am glad to say that I do not remember ever having eaten them myself. This is no way to treat sentient creatures.

As I grew older I would often be asked to fetch the cows from the field for milking which was done by hand. I would sometimes take my cup into the barn and squeeze one of the cow's teats if I wanted a drink of milk which I would now find quite revolting. The farm cats would all be waiting for their daily pinta at the end of the milking session, which was supplemented by anything they caught around the farm for themselves.

I once watched a cow give birth. She bellowed softly all the way through and as the calf slipped out she turned and started licking her all over. She struggled to her feet and began sucking straight away, but not for long. She would soon be taken away and put in a separate barn. The cow called endlessly for her calf but eventually gave up. Sometimes I was allowed to feed the calf with a bucket of substitute milk, and I had to put my fingers in her mouth so she could suck. Her tongue felt rough and slimy. I never thought to ask why she was not allowed to stay with her mother and have her milk but, of course, I now know that a calf is merely an unwanted by-product of the dairy industry, at least the male calf is. Females are mostly destined to follow their mothers into milk production. How did we ever become so cruel and insensitive – so arrogant as to assume that we have more right to a mother cow's milk than her baby has.

Professor John Webster of the Department of Veterinary Science at Bristol University said *"The most potentially distressing incident in the life of a dairy cow is the removal of her calf."*

Aunty Glad
and Uncle Tom

Jessie (right), me and friend

World War II Children's Home at Sennybridge

8

Starting school

I was so excited to be starting school and on the first day I was taken on foot for about a mile to the end of the country lane that led from Cilmanharen to the main road where I met up with one of our teachers and my sister Jessie. Then there was another half mile to walk to the school. It could not really be called a main road, cars were rarely seen and viewed as a sign of great prosperity. The school house was a grey Victorian building, now restored into a very attractive residential property alongside the river Honddu. There was only one classroom which was divided into two, one half for the Welsh children and their teacher and the other half for the evacuees and our teacher. I really enjoyed school and I think I did quite well at most of the lessons. After lunch, which consisted of our own packed sandwiches, folding canvas beds were brought out and the little ones were made to lie down for an hour, very often falling asleep, probably as a result of the long walk to school.

My second day at school involved Auntie taking me out of the farm gate on to the lane. She pointed in the direction of the main road and told me to keep walking until I met Miss Kenny, our teacher, at the end of the road. I thought I was never going to get there and started to panic as each bend in the lane failed to reveal any sign of the main road. Eventually I came in sight of my sister and ran to meet her with tears streaming down my face. We were so happy to be reunited that we chatted and skipped all the way to school.

At the end of the day when it was time to walk home I was again left at the end of the lane, this time by Miss

Kenny and my sister. I was told to keep walking until I reached Cilmanharen. I really did not want them to leave me and started to cry but with much persuasion I agreed to set off on my own. I had been walking for what seemed like eternity, praying that the next bend in the lane would reveal my destination. I wondered if I was going the right way, I didn't recognise anything. I came to a gate that led into a steep sloping field and at the top was a farm building. I wondered if it was Cilmanharen so I climbed over the gate. I hesitated as several sheep stopped grazing and were staring at me. I plucked up courage and started walking up the field. With one eye on the sheep and one on what I thought was my destination I continued. As I got closer I realized it was not Cilmanharen. I didn't know what to do. I noticed some of the sheep had come closer and my heart started thumping. I took a deep breath, opened my mouth and screamed as loud as I could over and over again scattering the sheep in all directions. I called 'Auntie, Auntie', but no one came. I realised that I must have gone the wrong way and started back down the field and out on to the lane again. Another half hour or so and to my relief I reached Cilmanharen. Auntie was pleased to see me but no one seemed surprised that I had managed to find my own way home and I don't know why I didn't tell them that I had lost my way. From then on the long lonely walks to and from school served to feed my imagination with all sorts of childhood fantasies. What games we would play when I got to school, who I would play with, what I would do in the little garden I had made at home and what I was going to give Bobby for tea. On the way home I would pick cowslips and buttercups, dandelions and daisies to make Bobby's table look pretty. In summer I would pick wild strawberries and thread them on a grass stalk. When I got home Auntie would put cream on them for my tea. No strawberries since have ever tasted so delicious. The miles of walking to and from school accounted for the sturdy studded boots we were made to wear.

The school taught both Welsh and evacuee children and I don't think the Welsh children were very happy about us common kids invading their territory. They taunted us and generally made us feel unwelcome. When I returned to Wales years later I met some of the boys, now grown up men, and we reminisced about old times. I could not believe they were the same people who teased us so mercilessly. They were so polite and shamefully embarrassed as we recalled various incidents that took place all those years ago.

I remember one incident very clearly. I was late coming out of school, having stayed behind to help the teacher. I could hear a terrible squawking noise. On the concrete balustrade of the bridge by the school was a jackdaw caught in a gin trap. His feet were trapped in the iron jaws of the trap and he was flapping his wings in an unsuccessful attempt to free himself. I started screaming, begging for someone to come and help to release him. With that, a group of boys about twelve years old came out from behind some bushes and started to laugh. I knew immediately that they had deliberately set the trap laced with food to catch any unsuspecting creature that alighted on it. In my anger I let out some unrepeatable expletives, not knowing that standing close behind me was one of the teachers. She completely ignored the unfortunate victim in the gin trap fighting to free himself as she grabbed my arm. She began telling me how disgusting I was to use such language and marched me to the washroom in the school building. Wondering what was going to happen to me I forgot about the poor bird. Still clutching my arm she told me to open my mouth, she was going to wash my mouth out. She ran the tap, let go of my arm, and rubbed soap on her hand. 'I hope this will be a lesson to you' she said and proceeded to put some frothy soap into my mouth. I instinctively spat it out as fast as I could and started to cry. With that she gave me a beaker of water and said 'Now rinse your mouth'. Thankfully, teachers would not be allowed to get away with such behaviour today.

Years later when I returned to Wales for a visit, there was a fete in the school hall. I was invited to attend and who should I see but the teacher who had washed my mouth out with soap and water, now elderly but unmistakable. I made a point of introducing myself and explaining how I went to the school as an evacuee. She did not admit to remembering me and I thought it prudent not to mention why I will always remember her. I don't know what happened to the unfortunate bird but it will always remind me how callous people can be.

Another time as I was walking home from school on my own, clutching my one and only precious book of children's stories, several boys aged about ten or eleven were lying in wait for me. They walked slowly towards me grinning sheepishly. I thought they were going to hit me but instead they asked me to show them my knickers. As I was backing away from them I held up my dress and revealed my grey flannelette knickers. I thought they would then leave me alone but instead one of the boys took down his trousers and revealed what was to be my first encounter with the male anatomy. As the boys came closer I said I was going to tell my teacher about them and as this did not do the trick I said if you leave me alone I will give you my book. One of the boys snatched the book and they all ran off. I never did tell anyone.

My parents paid us one fleeting visit during the seven years we were evacuated. I saw them for about ten minutes in the school playground. My only memory of that visit was my mother scowling and saying to me 'I see you are still biting your nails.' They gave us each a bag of boiled sweets that had all stuck together to form one large solid lump.

9
Bobby becomes Belinda

As I got older, Bobby, the teddy bear given to me by the WRVS when I was in Hastings, no longer appealed to me and I yearned for a real baby doll.

I was about eight years old when I went on a rare visit with Auntie Glad to the market town about six miles away. She had to get some wool and cottons from the haberdashery shop. As she was looking at the wool I was suddenly transfixed. Looking back at me from a glass cabinet under the counter was a doll's face, the moulded sort used for making rag dolls. I stared back and couldn't contain my excitement. I started to jump up and down. I looked at Auntie and she must have been swayed by the pleading look on my face as I pointed to the doll's face. 'What do you want that for' she asked. 'Make a dolly out of teddy' I said. Both Auntie and the shop assistant laughed. As she turned to ask the price I started to shake nervously, fearing that something would happen before I could actually see the assistant take it out of the cabinet and put it in my hand. Maybe Auntie would change her mind because it was too expensive or the lady in front of us would buy the only one left. I held my breath until, with ecstatic relief, I was finally clutching a brown paper bag containing the smiling face with big blue eyes and rosy cheeks. My baby was starting to come to life. In my mind I was already dressing her in hat, coat and bootees. I looked at Auntie with tears in my eyes and I clutched her hand tightly as a way of saying thank you. I couldn't wait to get home and start transforming teddy into the most beautiful baby doll. So with the help of

Auntie we cut off teddy's nose and ears, patched up the holes and sewed on the new face. We used some of Auntie's yellow wool to give him long blonde hair. When he was dressed in a pink bonnet to hide his scars and a lovely woollen coat and bootees he was no longer Bobby but Belinda, the most beautiful baby doll in all the world. Her cot was an old cardboard box on which I had painted flowers. Now all she needed was a pram so up into the granary I went where I had seen an assortment of old wheels and boxes as well as all manner of items like nails and wood. String was a vital ingredient and I knew there was masses of it in a big iron cauldron. I put my hand in and screamed out as a little mouse jumped out and landed in my lap. I jumped up, shook the mouse off and composed myself. Eventually I had all I needed for the task ahead. Lost in my world of fantasy and with great excitement I started to assemble Belinda's pram. Hours of intensive labour and it was finished. Heath Robinson would have been proud of me. I carried it down the granary steps and put it gently on the ground. I ran into the house to get Belinda and the little blankets and makeshift pillow I had made. As I laid her in her pram and put the blankets over her she looked so beautiful. Excitement filled my whole body and I was lost in my own little world of sheer joy. I got hold of the two sticks I had nailed to the side of the box for handles and gently started to push the pram. It worked beautifully and I walked around and around for several minutes proud of my achievement until one by one the wheels began to fall off. The disintegration of all my hard work became unbearable and I ran into the house crying and clutching Belinda reassuring her that I would try again tomorrow.

I can't remember birthdays but I do remember one Christmas when I sent a letter to Santa asking for a bike and a set of four knitting needles so I could practise knitting socks. I woke up Christmas morning to find he had left me the four knitting needles, a ball of wool and a prayer book. I don't really think I expected a bike so it was not such a great disappointment.

All the Welsh people I knew were very religious. Sundays involved church in the morning, Sunday school in the afternoon and chapel in the evening. Only essential tasks were undertaken on Sundays such as milking, cooking and feeding the animals. A bible was always within easy reach and since there were no other books I read it conscientiously without understanding a single word. A fortnightly concert was held in chapel after the service and I was encouraged to do my bit by singing or reciting. 'We plough the fields and scatter' and 'When Mothers of Salem' come to mind and I can still remember reciting a wartime poem called 'Mother doesn't Work' that went like this:

One day I met a little fellow playing in the street
His clothes were nicely patched and darned, his boots were strong and neat
His rosy face was full of smiles he knew no youthful cares
As I stopped and talked to him about his family affairs
And what's your father little man? 'Oh, father he works hard
And builds big battleships in a fine shipbuilding yard,
And sister Meg is in the WAAFS and Bill has gone to sea
Our family has all got work, 'cept Mother 'course and me
And doesn't Mother work? Oh no, he shook his curly head
No, Mother doesn't work, she stays at home all day, he said
I looked down on his little suit, well worn but trim and neat
Who mends your clothes my boy I asked, who cooks the meals you eat?
Why, Mother does of course he said, she made this suit of mine
She gives us scrumptious food to eat, Dad says her cooking's fine
So Mother's working hard I said while you're out here at play
He frowned – No! Mother doesn't work she stays at home all day.

I slept in a big double bed on a squashy feather mattress and crisp white cotton sheets. Cooking apples were stored for the winter on the wooden floor underneath the bed so it was like walking through an orchard on a damp autumn evening every time I went to bed. I would kneel by the bed every night to say my prayers and ask God to forgive me for all the bad things I had done during the day like telling small white lies, being rude to Auntie or thinking bad things about people. I was terrified of God, that all powerful man up in the sky who was watching everything I did and who would send me to hell and damnation if I did not behave myself. So I was always ready to ask his forgiveness even if I hadn't knowingly done anything wrong. 'Suffer little children to come unto me' he said. How could a God of love say such things? I didn't want to suffer even if it did mean I would go to heaven.

I do not now believe in any man-invented organised religions that I see as the cause of much dissent amongst us, and which gives licence to commit terrible atrocities in His name. Blaise Pascal said *'Men never do evil so completely and cheerfully as when they do it from religious conviction.'* Certainly, I think it is wrong to indoctrinate young children. I believe you can be a good person without religion. A respect for the world and all creation is the best I can do. I would like to think it is spiritual rather than religious, which is something one discovers oneself rather than being indoctrinated with someone else's beliefs.

Uncle Tom had six sons from his previous marriage and I can still recall the beautiful sound as they all sat around the fire harmonising whilst practising for the local male voice choir. Whenever I hear a Welsh male voice choir now I have such a feeling of nostalgia, especially when they sing *'We'll keep a welcome in the hillside, We'll keep a welcome in the Vales, This land you knew will still be singing, When you come home again to Wales.'* Whenever I heard it after I left Wales I used to imagine they were singing it especially for me.

Unlike adults, I don't think children reminisce about being happy or sad. They live for the moment and accept what life deals them day by day. I think the damage done to many children like evacuees was done in other ways that only surface later in life. Only those who have been raised without hugs and kisses, and the comfort and security of loving parents will understand what I mean. Mostly I didn't miss the hugs and kisses but I do remember being envious of Elizabeth who lived on a nearby farm and was the same age as me. I would sometimes walk the mile or so across the fields to play with her and I noticed the way her parents would fuss over her. One day her mother was making her a dress and I can remember wishing that she would make one for me. She sometimes made it obvious that she didn't like me very much. I remember one occasion quite clearly. She had invited some people to tea including Auntie, Uncle and me. I don't know if anyone else noticed but every time I helped myself to some jam or cake, as the other people were doing, she would move it away from me to the other end of the table. She made me feel so uncomfortable, like an outcast, which I suppose I was really.

Later in life, when I had my own two girls and adorable grandchildren I have realised what I missed and what is absent in any child's life if they have not had a loving and protective family life. It is a sense of belonging. I have never felt I belonged.

I do not regret having been sent away at an early age. I learnt far more about life than I would have done otherwise. Most of all I learnt how important it is for children to have loving parents who are always there for them no matter what and to have the ability to pass on that love to their own children. I read once that if one isn't loved as a child they are less likely to pass it on to their children. I am happy that I have proved them wrong.

10

Returning home

After the war when it was time for us to return home, a car came to take me to the railway station where I was to meet up with all the other evacuees returning home. I was excited and anxious at the same time. We boarded the train and were laughing and hanging out of the train windows, excited about the train journey. I was surprised to see Auntie walking down the platform towards me. She attempted a smile as she handed me a packet of dates for the journey. My laughter soon turned to tears as I realised that she was crying. "Don't forget to write to me will you bychen, let me know you are alright"? It really upset me to see Auntie cry and I suddenly felt it was all my fault because I was leaving her. "Yes, I will write to you and one day I will come back to see you Auntie". But it was another six years before I would see her again.

I was now twelve years old and I was on my way to live in an exciting big city where the 'streets were paved with gold'. They say 'it is better to travel than to arrive' and it certainly proved to be the case for me.

When I arrived home there were another three children in the family only to be followed a year later by one more. This time, to my father's delight it was a boy. Apart from Jessie I did not recognise any of my siblings and I only had a vague recollection of my parents. My mother must have been at her wits end wondering how on earth she was going to cope with seven children to feed and clothe on very little money all living in a tiny two bedroom flat in Deptford. I am sure this made her bitter and resentful towards us. I can never remember her smiling or being happy. I feared and hated her.

I had passed my Eleven Plus examination in Wales and on returning home I had gained a place at Greenwich Park Grammar School. My mother didn't like me going to the grammar school. She thought it was a bit above my station and she never ceased to remind me of where she thought I belonged. She didn't like me making myself look nice and berated me when I curled my hair.

I loved every minute I was at school. It was my escape. It was an all girls school where a strict uniform code had to be adhered to. We were never allowed out of school without our hats, ties and sashes. Felt hats in the winter and straw boaters in the summer. If anyone was caught eating or drinking in the street whilst wearing their school uniform they were up in front of the whole school in assembly the next morning and given a conduct order mark. I loved my school uniform because then I was like everyone else. I only had one white shirt so when it was dirty I would wash it out at night and often put it on the next morning while it was still damp. Free school meals and my subsidised uniform never ceased to remind me of my social status.

We were divided into houses named after famous women authors. I was very proud to be in Bronte house because I loved Jane Eyre. It was regarded as totally irresponsible to let your house down by obtaining bad marks, because each house was judged by the number of good and bad marks they had been awarded and the winner was announced in assembly at the end of each month.

Miss Carter, the headmistress, was very strict. She was a large plain woman with her hair drawn back into a bun. If girls met her in the corridors between lessons they would stop talking immediately and acknowledge her with a slight bow of the head as she passed. Nothing escaped her and on one occasion she called me to her office. I racked my brains wondering what I could have done wrong and knocked on her door with foreboding. As I entered her office she must have sensed my fear and almost immediately she changed from being the austere mistress of all she surveyed to a softly spoken caring person. She asked me how things were at home. I don't know if it was from sheer relief that I was not on the receiving end of her wrath, or the thought that someone actually cared about what happened at home, but I burst into tears and attempted to answer some of her questions. I never did discover what or how she knew about my family situation.

My spirits would rise as I closed the door behind me to go to school and sink when I returned home. Joyce, one of the youngest girls, would come in from school and sit in the corner of the room afraid to open her mouth. My father mockingly called her square-head, for no visible reason. I will always remember her look of sheer remorse as if apologizing for even existing. After our tea of two slices of bread and a scraping of jam, we would all wait in anticipation of being allowed to go out and play. We would go to the swings or just walk around the streets. Sometimes we would walk as far as the shops and pinch an apple or orange from a fruit stall. Other times we would bunk into the cinema or the bug hutch, as we called it, and watch such films as Roy Rogers and Trigger, Bambi, Lassie Come Home and National Velvet. It was magic, complete escapism. Sometimes we would stay in the cinema for hours and watch the films two or three times over just so we didn't have to go home. I remember coming out of the cinema into bright sunshine with a splitting headache and wondering what I was going to say for being out so long. I attempted to run away on several occasions, getting as far as the crossroads at the end of the road. Not knowing which way to go I returned home to face the music.

Once a week my mother would buy groceries which always included a bag of broken biscuits, not for us children, for her and my father. You got more to the pound if they were broken. The food cupboard was always padlocked but sometimes when we were really hungry at weekends, when there were no free school dinners, we found a way of getting the padlock off by bending one of the brass rings. We had done it so many times that eventually it broke. We were so frightened, we didn't touch the biscuits or anything else. When my mother came home there was all hell to pay and when the incident was relayed to my father we got the strap, which I am sure was just to appease my mother.

One day a man and a woman came to our house and said we were going to be taken into care. I pretended to feel upset and remorseful but secretly I was overjoyed that we were going to leave what was a very unhappy home life. But it was not to be. I was told that as I would soon be leaving school I would not be going with my three sisters. It would be some time before I would see my sisters again but we all exchanged letters and I knew they were happy. When they left school they all found good foster homes and went on to marry and have loving children of their own.

11

Starting work

Although I would have loved to have stayed on at school to take exams and go on to further education my mother said I needed to go out to work to support myself, and I suppose she was right really. So when I was sixteen I went to work in the City as a shorthand typist. My boss, a short, grey haired elderly man, would call me into his office to take dictation and thought that part of my duties was to let him fondle my breasts. Furthermore, a man who walked past my office window each day decided he would educate me in certain parts of the male anatomy. By that time I was beginning to wonder what sort of perverted place the City of London was. As I was very subservient and deferred to authority unquestioningly at that time, it took all my determination to pluck up courage and hand in my notice. I left, despite my boss offering me a substantial increase in salary.

My next job, near St Paul's Cathedral, was equally short lived since I couldn't get the hang of the Gestetner duplicating machine and got the sack.

Off to the employment agency again and a job in a small office in Queen Victoria Street. The only other female typist in the office resented me from the start and made my life unbearable. When she gave me typing to do she would literally throw it on my desk and never speak other than to find fault with my work. After only three weeks I went to the manager's office to hand in my notice. He was so apologetic when I told him the reason and didn't seem at all surprised which made me think that I was not her only victim. He explained that she had been with the firm a long time and was indispensable.

Shorthand typists were in great demand, and I got a job in an office in Newgate Street near the Old Bailey. The area was still very bomb-scarred but someone had made a pretty little garden near our office where we would sit and have our lunch. I was working for the chairman and his son and anyone else who wanted the odd bit of typing done. I loved my work and the people I worked with. I immediately fell head over heels in love with Raymond, the chairman's son. I went to pieces every time he called me into his office to take dictation. One of my jobs was to keep the drinks cabinet stocked up and the cigarette box topped up for when they had board meetings. Being unfamiliar with alcohol I don't know what the chairman thought when I asked him if he wanted soda water in his sherry.

One day Raymond came into my office and asked me if I would mind popping up to Harrods to collect some things for his wife. I did not know that he was married and it came as quite a shock. He must have noticed the surprised look on my face. I think he realised that I had feelings for him but never ever encouraged me or acknowledged it. He was such a gentleman and so handsome. I never stopped admiring him and I loved the little shopping trips to Harrods and Fortnum & Masons. I later realised that infatuation can wane as quickly as it starts so eventually I was able to control my feelings and stayed in the job for nine years until I was pregnant with my first baby.

Wedding Day

With orphaned lamb on returning to Wales

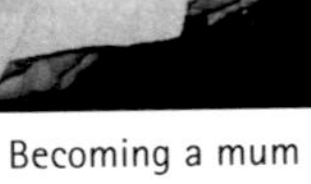

Becoming a mum

Me and Jilly

Christmas at the office

Happy families

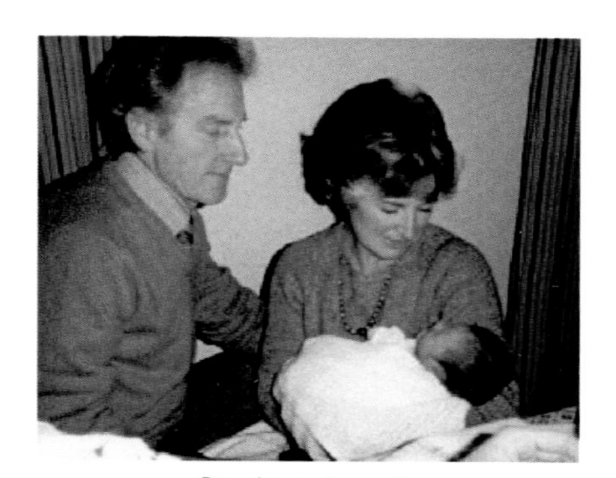

Proud grandparents

Golden Wedding Anniversary

12

Leaving home

When I was still only sixteen I was introduced to Maurice who was a friend of my aunt and uncle and quite a few years older than me. We started seeing each other, or as we called it then, 'courting'. I was not very experienced with the opposite sex and looking back I think I was just playing at being all grown up and in a relationship. Anyway I decided I would leave home and find somewhere to live on my own which was rarely heard of then, at least I did not know anyone who did it. I sought advice as to the legal age one could leave home and was told it was seventeen. I left on my seventeenth birthday amid a lot of verbal abuse from my mother.

I saw an advertisement for a room to let in New Cross at ten shillings a week. Being very naïve I accepted without even asking to see the room. When I arrived at the small terraced house the door was opened by a disheveled looking woman, her make-up still caked on from the night before - smudged mascara and lipstick reminiscent of a child who has raided her mother's make-up box. She invited me in and directed me to a small room off a dingy hall. There was just a small iron bedstead with crumpled bed-clothes on it. She suggested I made the bed myself and whilst doing so I felt so alone and sat on the bed to have a good cry. It started to get dark so I reached for the light switch but it did not come on. It was now about seven o'clock and Ann, the landlady had gone out. When it got to 10 o'clock and she still hadn't come back I decided to go to bed. In the morning I could hear her in the kitchen so I got up and told her that the light didn't come on and I had to sit in the dark all evening. She said, 'Oh, you should have put some money in the meter and she showed me how to do it. She told me in a roundabout way that she worked as a prostitute, so I only stayed one very cold night. The next day Maurice said I could come and stay at his parents' house. It was very kind of them to take me in but I didn't much like being a lodger. Although his parents and sister welcomed me I again felt like an outsider and always wary about doing the wrong thing. I wish I had been more confident and self assured in those days instead of accepting everything without question. A week after my eighteenth birthday Maurice and I married. I didn't know anything about how to organise a wedding. Maurice didn't want a lot of fuss so we booked the registrar's office. I ordered a big bouquet of red roses, a three-tier wedding cake in the shape of horseshoes and a big black chauffeured car. Three people turned up from my office, two of Maurice's friends and his mum. It poured with rain all day but I thought I was so grown-up, especially as I was now a wife. I don't know what I did with all that wedding cake.

I continued to commute to the City and enjoy the ups and downs of normal life until I gave birth to a beautiful baby girl five years later. So this was love. She was part of me, all mine, my very own family. Unlike today when new mums are often sent home the day after giving birth we stayed in the hospital for about ten days. The babies were put in the nursery and only brought out at feeding time. Sometimes when I heard the babies crying in the nursery I would strain my ears wondering if it was Jilly. I couldn't wait for feeding time to hold her close and feel her soft little face against my breast - the most precious time to bond with your baby. When I arrived home I would breast feed her every time she cried, relishing the opportunity for another cuddle. None of this four-hourly feeds as we were told to do.

When Jilly was nearly three years old I had to go out to work again and I found a part time secretarial job a few minutes from home. I managed to enroll her in a nursery which was part of a small private school for the three hours I was at work. I stayed in my job for eight years until we decided to move out of London to the Cambridgeshire countryside. 'New house, new baby' as they say, and this was no exception. I had another baby girl not long after we moved. We called her Lisa, another little bundle of joy. They have both enriched my life from the day they were born and I consider myself the luckiest mum in the world. Now that they are grown up with families of their own, another chapter in my life begins, that of being a proud grandmother of four.

13
Too little too late

Many years later I was to learn that there is a fine line between love and hate. By that time my mother was old and alone and I came to realise what a sad blow life had dealt her. I don't know if it was pity or love but I tried to forgive and forget the past as I held her hand in the care home where she sat in her favourite armchair surrounded by unresponsive strangers. Heaven help anyone who attempted to sit in her chair whilst she was out of the room. The only sound came from a flickering television to which no one was paying any attention. I looked around and dreaded the thought of ending my days like that. My Mother had given birth to eight children (one had died soon after birth) but only the youngest one and I visited her occasionally. They say you reap what you sow but sadly not everyone is skilled in the art of cultivation and should not be harshly judged if now and again the harvest fails. We are all victims of circumstances. Some of us get help along the way and have the determination to pull ourselves up. Others merely accept what life doles out to them and if you have had no education, as my mother hadn't, what chance do you have?

When my mother died I felt such sadness and regret that I had failed to recognise what a wretched and unfulfilled life she had had until it was too late. I regret that I did not persist in asking her about her childhood and her family. I suspect that all the anger and hostility she directed towards us was a reflection of what life had meted out to her. I once brought her home to spend Christmas with us but by the evening she was asking me to take her back. She had been in the care home for several years and I suspect the outside world was unfamiliar and frightening to her, and she felt safe in the care home.

I don't know if she chose to send us away at the start of the war or if she was coerced into it. I think that maybe she saw a way out of the struggle to bring up so many children with very little money or help. I do know of parents who refused to let their children go away to live with strangers unless they themselves went with them, and reading some of the stories that came out after the war about how some foster carers treated evacuees I can understand their concern. Whatever it was, it would be another six years before my mother would see five of her seven children again. Apart from one short meeting when my parents came to visit us in Wales they hardly knew us at all. Some of us went away mere babies and came back approaching our teenage years, speaking what sounded like another language having taken on the dialect of the part of the country to which we were sent. My parents were very amused by our Welsh accents. At my first school after returning to London I remember trying to recite a poem about a rat and being reduced to tears because, after several attempts, the closest I could get to 'rat' was 'rrrrrrut'.

We were strangers to our mother as she was to us. Apart from one sister, I had not seen or heard of any of my other siblings for six years. The bonding years were lost forever. My mother didn't know how to build bridges or open her heart to us, why should she, no-one had done so for her. I think she felt afraid and confused by the sudden onslaught of all these children demanding something she was unable to give.

Later in life when I had my own two children I wondered how society had allowed a whole generation of families to be torn apart, some never to be re-united, others to return to an alien and chaotic way of life that they could not adjust to, leaving them with a feeling of isolation and lost identity. When I have talked about this since the war, I have often been reassured that it was done for the children's own safety. Try telling that to the children who were not lucky enough to be billeted with a caring family. Many were physically and sexually abused. Some were treated like servants never being allowed to eat or socialise with the family.

14
Reunion

Several years ago I noticed a request on the letters page of my local newspaper. World War Two evacuees were invited to attend a reunion on Marylebone Station. One of the platforms had been especially commandeered for the purpose. My initial reaction was 'how exciting' and I began to make plans to go. However, as memories came flooding back the prospect became quite daunting. I walked from room to room trying to visualise what it would be like. Would I regret it if I didn't go, would I regret it if I did? At the very last minute I made up my mind to go and rushed around trying to get my things together. I arrived on Marylebone Station amid such a commotion of noise. A Vera Lynn look-a-like was singing "We'll Meet Again" accompanied by a 'Joe Loss' band. A vintage post office van and several wartime vehicles, together with women dressed in WRVS uniforms serving teas, set the scene of fifty years ago. Someone was making announcements over a microphone asking people to come forward if they had been evacuated from a certain London school to a particular part of the country, the idea being to reunite people. Hands were going up and people were invited to go up to the microphone in front of the television cameras and talk about their experiences.

There were about two hundred people there and as I stood taking in the atmosphere and looking around at all the people, I tried to imagine what they must have looked like fifty years ago and had they felt as I had and what effect it had had on them. Suddenly I heard the name of my school called and the destination South Wales. My hand shot up before I could help myself, but it was just as quickly retrieved as I realised I was now feeling quite emotional. My throat was tight and there was no way I would be able to talk on camera without crying. I walked away and stood apart from the crowd of people watching the proceedings when a man and woman came up to me and introduced themselves. He had been evacuated from the same London school to South Wales as I had. I explained my predicament and he said he quite understood so he and his wife invited me to join them for a coffee and a chat in the station restaurant. We seemed to talk for hours, and I learned that he had been billeted with a very nice family who had taught him all about farming, so much so that he was reluctant to leave it all behind and return to London. He was now a chauffeur and caretaker for a well-known celebrity.

On the way home I reminisced about the days' events, and I was glad I went, but sorry that I did not have the confidence to speak to some of the other ex-evacuees about their experiences.

With Spike Milligan at the opening of
new Animal Aid offices

15

Fighting injustice

With my girls now all grown up and independent, my mind turns once again to the plight of animal suffering and the animal rights movement. One of the issues at the time was to campaign against the export of live animals. Millions of lambs, poor worn out ewes, calves taken from their mothers at a few days old, and many other animals were being herded on to lorries to travel hundreds of miles across Europe, sometimes as far afield as the barbaric slaughterhouses in Spain and Italy or, in the case of the tiny calves, to continental veal crates. The lucky ones were dead on arrival.

One of the protests against live exports involved civil disobedience. We made a pledge to a well-known celebrity to take part in a sit-in on the main road to Dover Docks. The public needed to know about this despicable trade. It was very emotional as two hundred of us sat down and linked arms and refused to move even when cautioned that we would be arrested. One by one we were hurled off the road. A big burly police officer grabbed my arm, cautioned me and dragged me to 'the wagon'. I was locked in a very small compartment resembling a cupboard and it was then I realised that I might be claustrophobic. There was a tiny window high up so I stood on the bench and concentrated on the scene outside so as not to feel so confined. I watched as fellow protesters were being brought in and put into wagons. Those who decided they were not going to co-operate would go completely limp and were being dragged along by two officers. After about four hours in the wagon I was taken out and put into a police cell where I was re-united with other protesters. The ordeal became one of a united front against the atrocities meted out to animals every day.

My day in court was not so daunting. A kindly judge fined me £40 and regretted that I 'now had a criminal record'. Mustering up all my courage I said, "I do not consider myself a criminal, the criminals are out there abusing animals", to which he gave a little smile and said "That's as maybe, you are free to go".

My next encounter with the law came during an outbreak of ecoli which was blamed partly on dirty slaughterhouses resulting in contaminated meat. Douglas Hogg, the then Agricultural Minister, was to give a speech in the House of Commons about it. Myself and two friends made our way to the public gallery to listen to him. During his address, he mentioned the amount of faeces on the floors of the slaughterhouses. With that, Tony Banks (staunch advocate for animal rights) jumped up and reminded Douglas Hogg that he would shit himself too if he was queuing up to have his throat cut. We had positioned ourselves in the public gallery so that we were able to make our point, albeit not quite as we had planned. Nevertheless, we stood up and cheered, *'Well done Tony – stop the slaughter'.* There was such a commotion as two burly security men grabbed us and took us down to the cells where some kindly police officers made us a cup of tea and told us we would have to wait until the Speaker of the House, Betty Boothroyd, gave permission for us to be released. We didn't have to wait long.

The following quotation by Henry Beston sums up for me where we have gone wrong in our attitude to animals. *"We need another and a wiser and perhaps a more mystical concept of animals. We patronize them for their incompleteness, for their tragic fate of having taken form so far below ourselves. And therein we err, and greatly err. For the animal shall not be measured by man. In a world older and more complete than ours they move finished and complete, gifted with extensions of the senses we have lost or never attained, living by voices we shall never hear. They are not brethren, they are not underlings; they are other nations caught with ourselves in the net of life and time, fellow prisoners of the splendour and travail of the earth."*

I think, looking back and remembering my life at home in Deptford, I could understand and relate to how animals felt when they were maltreated. I wanted them to know that I was their friend and I would try to protect them, but of course it was not possible. I was met with derision when I tried to stop someone drowning kittens, castrating lambs or ringing pig's noses, and when they killed a chicken by ramming a knife down her throat and swinging her by the legs until her little body surrendered the last drop of blood, I would go and hide somewhere to cry. That was no way to treat living sentient creatures.

I now devote much of my time exposing what goes on behind the closed doors of vivisection laboratories, factory farms, slaughterhouses, zoos, circuses, on shooting estates etc. In fact, I have spoken out wherever man, in his endeavour to dominate the whole of creation, has caused so much pain and misery. I did not have the option of turning away. Has it been worthwhile? I would like to think so.

With Joanna Lumley, Martin Shaw and Susan Jameson at a Compassion in World Farming demonstration

16

Final chapter

Now aged seventy four I have tried to give my girls and my grandchildren an insight into my early life before they came along to change and enrich it forever. I hope they are not disappointed.

I have tried to show them, by example, to have respect for all life. Animals, like us, are sentient beings with most of the same feelings and emotions and should be treated with the same consideration in relation to their needs.

And they have taught me that *'Love is a many splendoured thing'.*

A short while ago I was diagnosed with motor neurone disease. I wish I could have spared them that. At this most difficult time I try to find strength through the love of my family and friends and the support of the medical profession, to cherish each day for as long as I can.

The way to judge if your life has been worthwhile is to know that you are loved.